IMAGES
of America

EL PASO
1850–1950

IMAGES
of America

EL PASO
1850–1950

James R. Murphy

ARCADIA
PUBLISHING

Published by Arcadia Publishing
Charleston, South Carolina

Library of Congress Control Number: 2009922903

For all general information contact Arcadia Publishing at:
Telephone 843-853-2070
Fax 843-853-0044
E-mail sales@arcadiapublishing.com
For customer service and orders:
Toll-Free 1-888-313-2665

Visit us on the Internet at www.arcadiapublishing.com

*This book is dedicated to my wife, Margarita, and my son, Ian;
both have been, and continue to be, my inspiration.
It is because of their patience and uncompromising love that
I have been fortunate to "test" many of my daydreams
and because of them that I am allowed to walk
the less familiar path with confidence.*

CONTENTS

ACKNOWLEDGMENTS

I first want to thank El Paso Museum of History's former director Jennifer E. Nielsen for allowing me to serve as the museum development director; this changed everything. I will also acknowledge museum senior curator Barbara Angus. When Arcadia Publishing first presented me with this opportunity, I walked right over to Barb's office and sought her approval.

Claudia Rivers, head of the University of Texas at El Paso (UTEP) Special Collections, was very inviting. Over the weeks that followed, I scoured more than 6,000 of the library's photographs. Image specialist Yvette Delgado, along with everyone in Special Collections, was very polite and patient.

After combing through UTEP's photographs, I turned to El Paso Public Library's director Carol Brey-Casiano and Border Heritage librarian Marta Estrada. She, too, was very calming and patient. The library's Claudia Ramirez scanned dozens and dozens of photographs for me with help from Ruth Brown . . . thank you.

Without the City of El Paso's historic preservation officer Dr. Troy Ainsworth's detailed analysis of the architecture presented in chapter four, there would be no chapter four. Here's to ya, Laddie!

I will also acknowledge Dr. Marc Thompson and Dr. Oscar Martinez for their assistance; Patricia Worthington from the El Paso County Historical Society; Ian Edwards and Steve Lloyd for being my lifelong inspirations, and the former staff at the Cultural Resources Council of Syracuse and Onondaga County and Laurie Reed in Syracuse, New York. Most importantly, I want to thank my dad, Robert F., for teaching me to work hard and not to be afraid to admit it when I am wrong. And, of course, thanks to my mom, Betty (Lizbit), who is the nicest person one will ever meet, cool like a cucumber. My parents gave to their children the foundation necessary to make common sense decisions, never denying us the freedom of choice.

On a final note: one time in the seventh grade, I did not turn in an assignment. Mr. Niles gave me time to make it up. I still did not do the work. He called me up to his desk and stated, "Murphy, you will never finish anything!" Ever since then, I have finished everything.

Life is great! Don't give up!

INTRODUCTION

El Paso, Texas, is located in the far western tip of Texas and is sometimes referred to as the forgotten stepson of Texas—loved but not paid much attention to. Immediately to the north is the state of New Mexico, and immediately to the south, on the other side of the Rio Grande, is the country of Mexico.

Evidence of tribal life in this region dates back some 13,000 years. Written history dates back more than 400 years. The first Thanksgiving in North America was held here. According to author W. H. Timmons, "Álvar Núñez Cabeza de Vaca and his three companions, survivors of an unsuccessful Spanish expedition to Florida, may have passed through the El Paso area in 1535. In 1540–42, an expedition under Francisco Vázquez de Coronado explored an enormous amount of territory now known as the American Southwest. The first party of Spaniards that certainly saw the Pass of the North (El Paso del Norte) was the 1581 Rodríguez-Sánchez expedition." Juan de Oñate took control of the area in 1598.

In 2007, sculptor John Houser's *Equestrian* was installed at the El Paso International Airport. It is reportedly the largest equestrian bronze in the world. It is by all accounts a tribute to Oñate, but such fervor came from the Native Americans and others that lay claim to Oñate being a ruthless torturer and killer, the statue's name was changed, and the location was moved from the original choice, next to the El Paso Museum of History in plain sight, to where it is now, hidden at the entrance to the El Paso International Airport.

The people of El Paso, because of its close ties to Mexico, are predominantly Mexican, or Hispanic as they prefer to be called. In a uniquely odd fashion, many Hispanics (American-born Mexicans) are quick to denounce their kinship to Mexicans just across the border. There is an apparent exclusivity in being American born. This is not limited to El Paso; denouncing people of the same ilk has been common in many other countries around the world pretty much forever. While Hispanic El Pasoans are quick to denounce their brethren, they are also just as quick to protect them in their wish for a more democratized life.

It is interesting how this once tiny Mexican settlement joined together by a river's resources grew into the international crossroads formally divided by that same river. Even today, El Paso, in so many ways, is a sleepy little town still trying to find its place among the more progressive U.S. cities. El Paso is quaintly 20 years behind the times. Wheeling and dealing through the back door is still commonplace. Tons of illegal drugs come into this country every week. Tons are taken into custody. Tons make it through. Illegal aliens work in this border town by the thousands: cleaning executives' homes, doing yard work, building homes, working in establishments all throughout the city, and no one does as much as raise an eyebrow. Politicians who take the time to visit El Paso are never given the opportunity to "see" El Paso and get a glimpse of its people and true way of life. They are shuffled around, courted to, and then shuffled off back to the airport. No visitor can acquire the magnitude of El Paso border issues and border life without remaining here for at least a little while. If any visitor were to walk from I-10 to the International Bridge (maybe 1 mile away), walk across the footbridge into Mexico and walk back across, they would learn much in that simple, two-hour time frame. If they were to do it by themselves, they would return a changed person and perhaps then be somewhat awakened.

What I have attempted to accomplish in my book is as much of an in-depth history through photographs and text as one could. In chapter one, "Life Along the Ro Grande," I provide a glimpse into El Paso's past beginning with the very basics and lead up to the period of tremendous change in the late 1800s. There is no turning back from this point forward. In chapter two, "Birth of a City," buildings, parks, electricity, and automobiles are becoming commonplace; the trolley system is replaced, leading to the retirement of trolley-puller Mandy the Mule. In "Business," I start with the cattle industry, but one begins to see the immediate emergence of a boomtown created by the arrival of the railroad, as well as the names of people, businesses, and organizations, the good and the bad, that created the foundation for a border community with laws and regulations that provided the impetus for El Paso as it is today. Chapter four, "Architecture," details the builders and buildings I found interesting. As I drive through El Paso, it is amazing to see so many landmark structures from that era gone by alongside or in a neighborhood with adobe buildings and homes. I would love to have extended the text throughout chapter five, "Mexican Revolution," but could not. My hope is to pique your curiosity enough so that you continue research on your own. Many important people and characters came to the forefront during the Mexican Revolution in a relatively short period of time—killings, assassinations, double crossings—and in essence, not much has changed 100 years later. In chapter six, I briefly examine the "Military." The U.S. military and the Border Patrol learned and developed a great deal from their confrontational border experiences in Texas. Chapter seven dives into the world of "Sports": bullfighting, cockfighting, boxing, gambling, baseball, rodeos, and other sporting events. Chapter eight, "People/Business/Health," is not so much about individual people, although a few are pinpointed; it is about groups of people, most doing good deeds and others not so good. But these elements are what join to make a city's history. Am I right?

One

LIFE ON THE RIO GRANDE

Life along the Rio Grande was not always a pleasant experience. Many lived a life of near squalor with little protection from the elements. While at times the Rio Grande provided valuable resources, more than occasional flooding or the drying up of the river attributed to a consistently unknown future.

Due to the reality that there were few natural building materials such as wood, early settlers began a process of making shelters of adobe brick. A mixture of clay, sand, and water is baked by the intense heat of the sun, turning the mixture almost as hard as concrete. The adobe outdoor oven, or horno as it is known, pictured just left of the home, is used to bake bread and tortillas.

Smeltertown was built in the 1880s by workers of the Kansas City Consolidated Smelting and Refining Company, later renamed American Smelting and Refining Company, or ASARCO as it is still known today. Smeltertown lies between downtown El Paso and the upscale west side of the Franklin Mountains. Undue lead absorption in a high percentage of area schoolchildren and adults eventually led to the closing of ASARCO and Smeltertown's demolition.

This picture portrays the Elephant Butte Dam dedication ceremony in Elephant Butte, New Mexico. There were so many man-made canals feeding off the Rio Grande north of the Texas state line that, by the time the river reached El Paso, there was not enough water left for irrigation, leaving many of the crops dead by the middle of the long, hot border region's summer. When completed in 1916, it was the largest man-made reservoir in the United States.

Acequias (irrigation ditches) fed water to farmlands in El Paso dating back to the 1800s. During the mid-1880s, when the region's population began to rapidly increase, the irrigation system that once served the farms proved inadequate. Private companies eventually built the system that intertwines throughout El Paso today, providing a large percentage of lower valley homes with plentiful water for green lawns and shade trees during spring, summer, and fall.

The word *acequias* originally came from the Arabic *as-saquiya* (water carrier). The earliest knowledge of *acequias* in Texas was dug near Ysleta around 1680, east of downtown but still in El Paso County. These ditches that thematically traverse throughout El Paso, usually behind one's home, remain dry throughout late fall and winter. When spring arrives, the canals are flooded with water every third week for the next 33 weeks. Homeowners open access-ports, allowing water to flood front and back yards.

The Rio Grande Reclamation Project provides water for 69,010 acres of land. There are more than 350 miles of canals and laterals, and more than 2,205 turnouts, irrigating crops of cotton, alfalfa, pecans, chilies, family gardens, and more. The Rio Grande Project was operated and maintained by the U.S. Bureau of Reclamation until 1980, when the El Paso County Water Improvement took over.

Pictured above is the mule car Travias de Ciudad Juárez (Travel to the City of Juárez). A day excursion into Mexico from the United Sates has always been high on the list of tourists, as one can see by these well-dressed men and women ready to board the mule-drawn trolley. Many El Pasoans remember stories about Mandy the Mule, who pulled the trolley through the city and across the wooden-framed International Bridge into Juárez.

Catching a fish on the Rio Grande in El Paso is not practiced as much today as it used to be. In this photograph, a young woman pulls an 8-inch fish from the river on her long, branch-style fishing pole, probably borrowed from one of the boys. The Rio's water is swifter than one might imagine and can be extremely dangerous. But in this photograph, the day is sunny and the fishing is good.

Cantaloupe, avocado, and much more always taste better out of the back of a truck. Even today in some El Paso supermarkets, one can purchase fruit and vegetables grown in neighboring Mexico. In the fall season, stores roast fresh chili outside their front doors and sell it by the pound. Some believe that the Mexican produce is fresher and better tasting as a result of the lack of chemicals and additives used. (Courtesy of University of Texas at El Paso, C. L. Sonnichsen Special Collections.)

The span between El Paso and Juárez is much larger today, and the water level is lower than in this photograph. Today the International Bridge hangs high above the river with millions of people crossing into El Paso annually. The taming of the Rio Grande and multiple fences that have been built to deter illegal immigrants have dramatically changed this peaceful vantage point from when goods and people crossed at will. (Courtesy of University of Texas at El Paso, C. L. Sonnichsen Special Collections.)

Engine No. 1, El Paso & Southwestern Railroad

In this photograph, one can see the dramatic growth in ingenuity and design elements that the railroad industry engaged in over a relatively short period of time. El Paso's Engine No. 1 (in the forefront), a 19th-century 4-4-0 locomotive, was built in 1857 by the Breese and Kneeland Company. The Milwaukee Railroad sold it to what would soon become the El Paso and Southwestern Railroad (EP&SW). Engine No. 1 was the EP&SW's first train. It appeared in the 1938 film *Let Freedom Ring*. After it retired from service, it was positioned at the Centennial Museum on the UTEP campus for more than 40 years. In 1960, restoration began, and the engine can now be seen at the Railroad Transportation Museum near downtown El Paso's Union Depot.

Enjoying an afternoon in the park has been and still is a family affair in El Paso. This beautiful 1910 photograph is enticing. Thanks to El Paso's unbeatable, year-round sunshine, thousands of El Pasoans make the trek to the park of their choice every weekend. (Courtesy of University of Texas at El Paso, C. L. Sonnichsen Special Collections.)

According to March 10, 1893, city council minutes, the city purchased land from the El Paso County Fair Association for $66. The parcel was named Washington Park. Tony Carvajal, a young man who lost his left leg in a train accident, eventually worked as a lifeguard at the park. Park officials claimed Carvajal was the only lifeguard with one leg in the country. He saved nine swimmers' lives in one summer. (Courtesy of University of El Paso Library Special Collections.)

In 1901, the city council considered selling Washington Park to retired El Paso County sheriff James H. Boone, but instead, siding with public opinion, the land was leased to Boone for 20 years. Boone made major improvements to the park, lived on the grounds, and managed it for 13 years before his death. (Courtesy of University of El Paso Library Special Collections.)

If the readers look closely, they can see an automobile inside the Trost and Trost–designed Alhambra Theater on South El Paso Street during the 1930s. The crowd of mostly men attends this evening auto show, providing a glimpse of the year's latest automobiles.

In this 1915 view looking northwest into El Paso, the city is growing by leaps and bounds. The 7,192-foot-tall North Franklin peak looms in the dusty background. A mix of modern homes and businesses lines the streets. The conceptual rise of livable and work-sustaining structures defines a city. Without creative, well-built homes and businesses to protect its people, machinery, and sellable goods, a community cannot prosper. In El Paso, where harsh winds can blow for days on end at times with so much desert dirt in the air the sky can resemble a northern state's snow-driven "white-out" with zero visibility. Protection from the elements as in extreme cold is equally necessary in extreme heat. (Courtesy of University of Texas at El Paso, C. L. Sonnichsen Special Collections.)

Two

Birth of a City

El Paso's Boot Hill, Concordia Cemetery, is located at 3700 Yandell Street. There are more than 60,000 people buried in Concordia Cemetery, including gunslinger John Wesley Hardin, early Mormon pioneers, Civil War veterans, buffalo soldiers, Texas Rangers, and numerous other civic leaders, pioneers, and war veterans. It is the largest cemetery in the Southwest at 52 acres. By 1890, sections were purchased by various ethnic and religious groups and designated black, Catholic, Chinese, Jesuit, Jewish, Masonic, military, city, and county. (Courtesy of Concordia Heritage Association.)

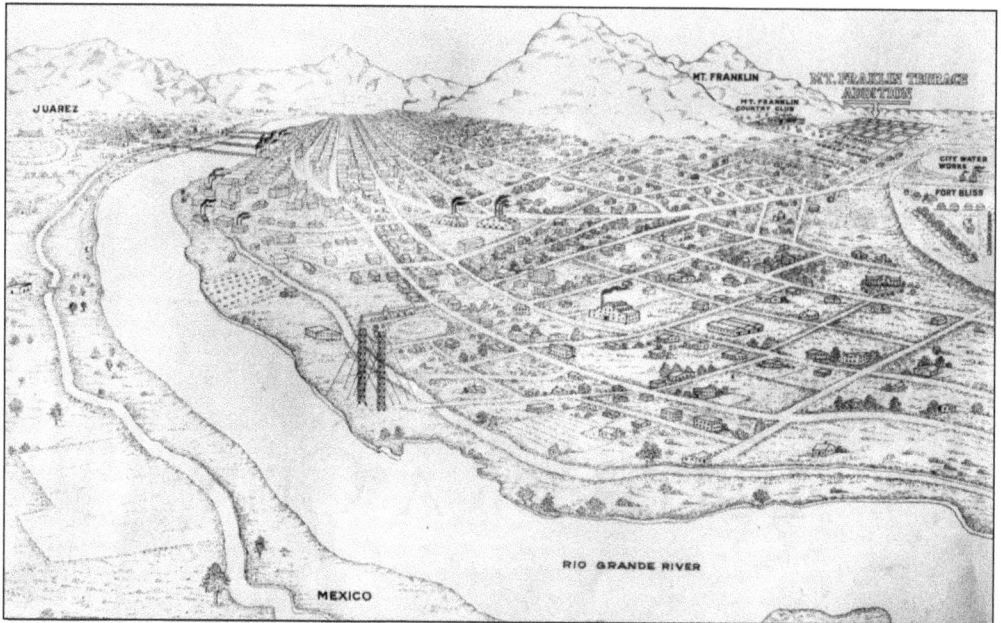

In this International Engraving Company plat map, four bridges cross into Juárez, Mexico, and another is under construction. Civilization has crept to the base of the Franklin Mountains. The Mount Franklin Terrace Addition and Mount Franklin Country Club stand in the distance, and Fort Bliss is present. The farmland in the center of the map has long since disappeared. The little burrow of Juárez is now twice the size of El Paso.

In the late 1800s, a collection of individuals led by Gen. Anson Mills acquired a charter for the El Paso Street Railway Company and soon began the operation of a mule-drawn streetcar system. As El Paso grew, it desired more modern conveniences. With that came the installation of electric lighting and electric streetcars. Mandy the Mule lost her job in 1902 when new electric cars were put into service.

20

J. Fisher Satterwaite was an El Paso politician. He is responsible for Mesa Gardens, a popular establishment where people gathered to socialize. As can be seen in this bird's-eye view from Mesa Gardens, it was an ideal location for dancing, shuffleboard, eventually a zoological garden, a museum, a billboard hall, a shooting gallery, and a cold beer. It closed its doors near the end of the Mexican Revolution.

J. Fisher Satterwaite was also responsible for the makeover of San Jacinto Plaza. He planted trees, erected fountains, and even had live alligators placed in the pond. The plaza has been acknowledged as La Placita, La Plaza, and La Plaza de los Largartos (the Plaza of the Alligators). It has served as the center of downtown for more than 100 years and remains a gathering place for today's older generation, with many still donning their cowboy hats and boots.

Peter Kern had a dream for the property deemed Kern Place. He arrived in El Paso in 1881, around the same time the railroad arrived. In 1916, in an attempt to sell homes, he had this intricate, artful entrance designed. There were 444 electric lights illuminating Kern Place. Many nearby neighbors complained because of the brightness of the bulbs. The gate was taken down in 1954 for a street-widening project.

Named after Pres. Grover Cleveland, Cleveland Square was the gathering place for a meeting between William Howard Taft and Porfirio Diaz. This would mark the first time U.S. and Mexican presidents had ever met. Today the new El Paso Museum of History and the newly renovated El Paso Public Library rest on the north and east perimeter of Cleveland Square.

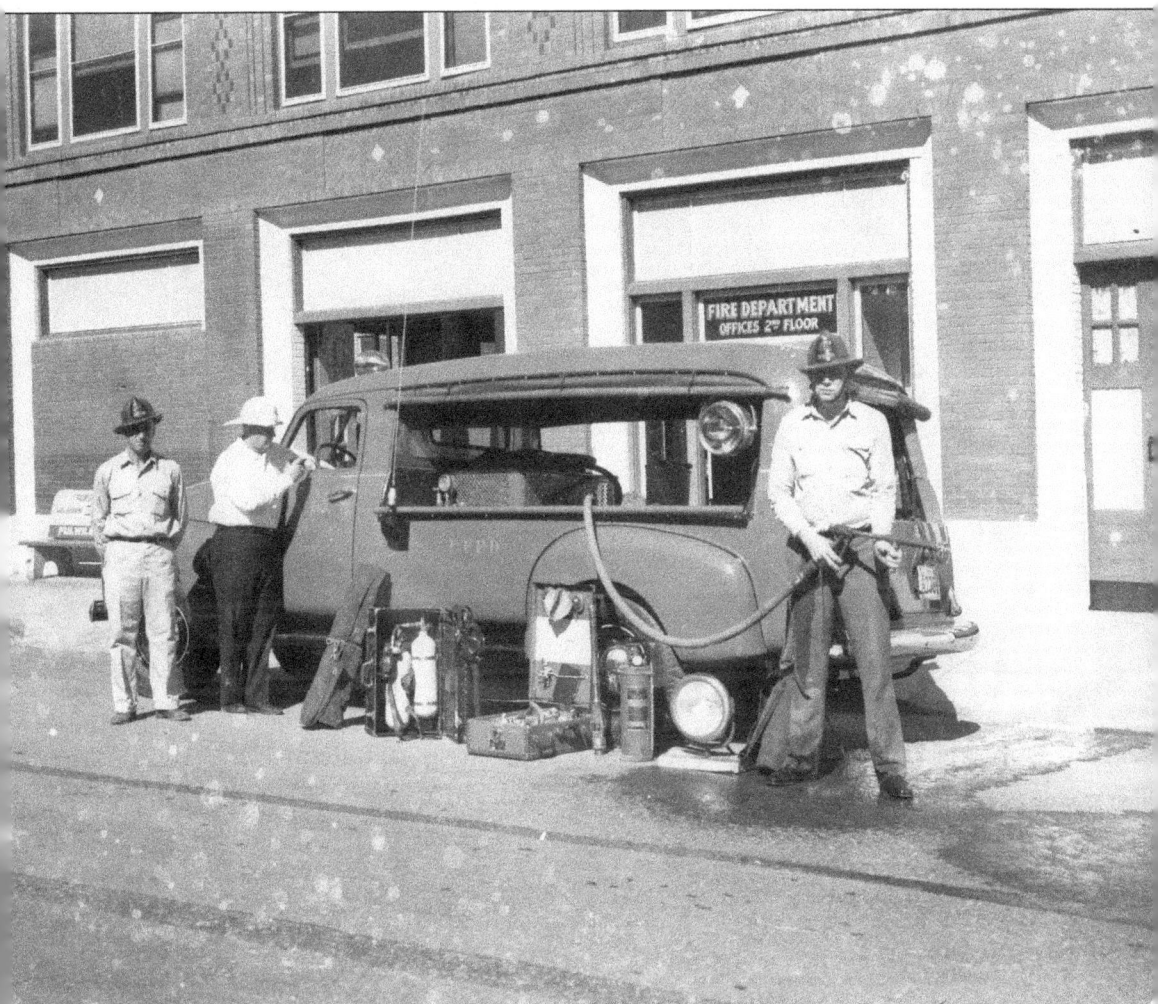

Like all little towns, El Paso depended on bucket brigades to douse fires. In 1881, a shed at the Overland Mail Company caught fire. It was the first real fire to cause great concern. The shortcomings of the bucket brigade became clear. By 1890, the El Paso Fire Department consisted of a single hook-and-ladder company and three hose companies. Since the water came from wells dug in the Rio Grande, when the river dried up, there was no water. Pomeroy's El Paso Transfer Company suffered $25,000 worth of damage because water pressure was inadequate. A second fire obliterated the "pride" of El Paso—the Grand Central Hotel. Built in 1883, it was the social center of the city. The four-story hotel was notably the most magnificent throughout the Southwest. On February 11, 1892, after burning for 11 hours, it was completely destroyed. The city council eventually agreed to supply the company with carts, hose reels, and 1,000 feet of hose. However, they did not keep their promise and supplied only 100 feet of hose.

When the railroads arrived in 1881, El Paso flourished. First it was the Southern Pacific and then the Santa Fe. In 1880, it is estimated that the town had close to 1,000 citizens. By 1890, this estimation grew to 10,338. Miners, farmers, merchants, real estate brokers, and all walks of regular life, the decent and the naughty, flocked to El Paso. Saloons popped up, and gambling was popular, as was prostitution.

This beautiful picture represents the inevitable changing of the times; modern times verses the soon-to-be past. A wagon, the main form of transport for centuries, still serves a useful and affordable means of transferring family members and goods. The automobile, on the other hand, provides a much quicker form of travel.

24

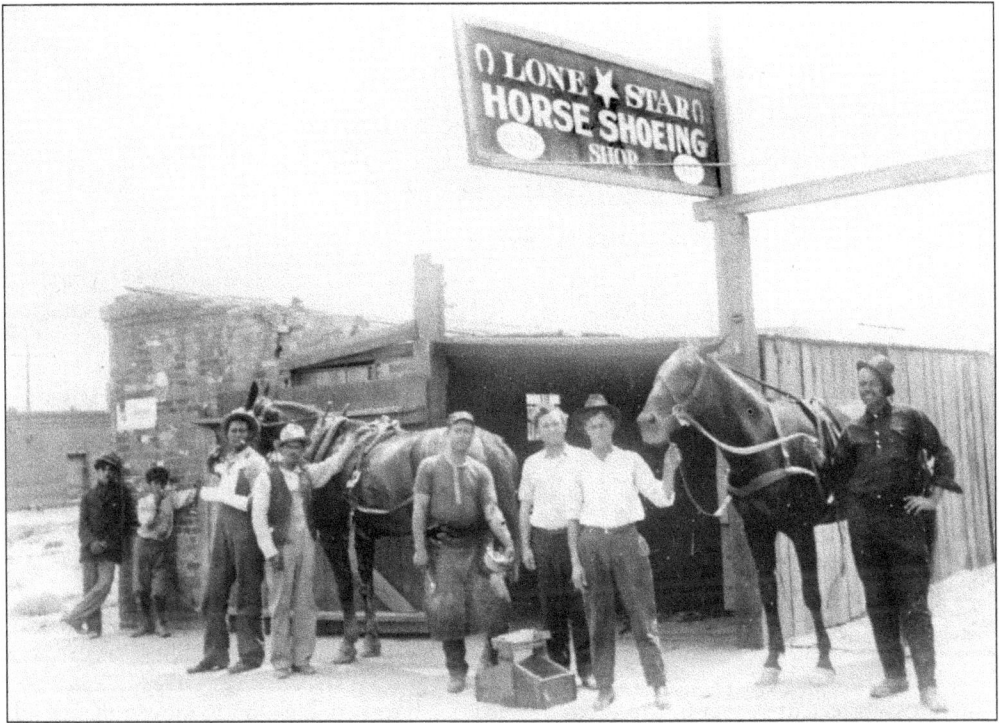

Naturally, before and during the transitional period between the "Real West" leading into the mechanized world in which El Paso now resides, horseshoeing and blacksmithing were essential businesses.

Notice the electric trolley line over the International Bridge looking toward Juárez, Mexico, and the bilingual stop sign. The bridge allowed for a massive influx of people into El Paso who lived in deplorable conditions in Chihuahuita (El Paso's First Ward), along the Rio Grande. Overcrowding, inadequate sanitation, and poorly built adobe structures led to the ultimate demolition of much of Chihuahuita.

The El Paso streetcar system in the 1920s traveled north to Fort Bliss, on to Government Hill, Highland Park, the Second Ward (El Segundo Barrio), and Juárez. There was also the Interurban line from downtown, east to Ysleta. Streetcars were host to numerous problems, one being an overloaded circuit. This would cause the car to immediately stop in its tracks, throwing the passengers forward. Buses began replacing trolleys in 1925.

Mother Praxedes Carty had been superior general of the Sisters of Loretto before her appointment to El Paso in 1922 as local superior. She was well known as a builder. El Pasoan Henry Trost was entrusted with drawing up plans for the new Loretto Academy. The facility opened its doors to students in September 1923. The buildings face Mexico and reach out in a welcoming gesture.

Alzina DeGroff purchased the Vendome Hotel in 1899. She renamed it Hotel Orndorff after her second husband. In 1924, she borrowed $825,000 to design a new hotel at a cost of more than $1.4 million. DeGroff passed before the building was completed. In 1935, the name was changed to the Hotel Cortez, where, according to the Warren Report, Pres. John F. Kennedy's plans to visit Dallas were laid. He was assassinated five months later.

On the corner of North Mesa and Mills Streets, a policeman is seen directing traffic with a pivoting "stop and go" sign. In the window of the auto on the left, a sign reads "Arizona" with some numbers underneath. Is this an early license plate? The auto to the right presents an early form of mobile advertising: "Maxwell, The World Champion." Hotel Orndorff is in the background.

The Sun Bowl was chartered in 1934, making it the second oldest college bowl game. In 1936, the game featured Hardin Simmons University and New Mexico State University. It began with a parade and the crowning of a queen. This State National Bank float exemplifies the bank's prominent role in the El Paso business community since its founding in March 1881.

Over the years, the Sun Carnival has undergone many changes. In its heyday, the parade featured hundreds of participants, including top-notch bands and beautifully decorated floats. The Thanksgiving Day parade is now shorter in length with few out-of-town groups. Choosing the Sun Carnival Queen has been modified a number of times. Today, judges known to a select few, monitor contenders during the Sun Bowl festivities prior to naming a winner.

Three

BUSINESS

As early as the 1830s, cattle were being driven from Texas to surrounding states. In 1866, Texans drove more than 260,000 cattle to assorted markets. Charles Goodnight is credited with inventing the chuck wagon in 1866 while preparing a cattle drive from near Fort Belknap in north Texas to Denver. The chuck wagon served as a social center where the tales of the day were told.

In 1881, Ernst Kohlberg opened a wholesale and retail cigar store. Joined by his brother Moritz, he operated the business under the name of Kohlberg Brothers Tobacco Company. Five years later, they opened the International Cigar Factory. As the first cigar manufacturers in the Southwest, their signature product was the popular La Internacional cigar. The business was located at 115 South El Paso Street.

Originally an orphan from the state of Vermont, Oscar T. (O. T.) Bassett's biggest investment was his lumberyard on the corner of Stanton and North Mills Streets. For a year and a half, Bassett could not keep up with the growing demand for lumber and accessories from his yard. Once the railroads were established, business grew briskly from Texas to California. It was Bassett's lumber that built El Paso.

Lumber, while not readily available in the desert of the Southwest, became a necessary ingredient when the population began to explode in the late 19th century. Loads of milled lumber began arriving, mainly from the Cloudcroft, New Mexico, area.

On February 15, 1886, the new El Paso County Courthouse was dedicated. Two alabaster statues of women holding balancing scales, called *Blind Justice*, were placed on top of the three-story building. Coal- and wood-burning stoves provided heat in winter months. All of the ceilings were 15 feet high, and the walnut staircases were all 6 feet wide. Brand-new autos adorn the front of the building on this winter's day.

The above unidentified carriage shop is believed to be either Noakes Carriage Company or S. D. Myers Saddlery. In 1930, the *El Paso Times* posted an article detailing a U.S. Census Bureau report stating that El Paso grossed $107 billion in retail and wholesale business dealings. Some 25¢ out of every dollar came through stores and services in the automobile industry. This was $3.6 million more than El Pasoans spent on groceries.

According to a 1902 *El Paso Herald* article, the first automobile was brought to El Paso by Frank Bell in the spring of 1902 and was destroyed by fire a short time afterward. By 1909, the *Herald* states there were more than 400 automobiles and plenty of good roads. The Christy Auto Company was an early dealer.

In east El Paso, down in the Lower Valley in 1909, there were 21 miles of paved road surface that made its way east to San Elizario. The *El Paso Herald* notes that a government expert said, "This is one of the finest roads in the country." Tires were stacked up in this unidentified El Paso business just waiting to be placed on the next vehicle.

In 1906, Stanton Street became the first paved street in El Paso. In 1907, the first automobile license in El Paso was issued to Dr. Frank Thatcher. In 1912, the first truck licensed was a Ford. In 1917, the State of Texas began issuing licenses. Velle Pleasure Cars was in the middle of it all.

In 1917, some 8,400 automobiles were registered in El Paso County. In 1923, the speed limit was increased from 25 miles per hour to 35. In 1922, there were 18,851 automobiles registered. In this photograph of J. R. Turner's full-service station, the business sells gas and tires, and has a complete repair shop. On this day, there is even a car being serviced on the outdoor lift.

El Paso's many bakeries still flourish even today, baking delicious, traditional Mexican pastries such as empanadas, esponjas, galletas de grajeas, marranitos, pan dulces, payasos, Protestante con pastas, simon, and many more varieties. Snowflake Bakery, in the above photograph, is in full swing with wagons ready to make the morning deliveries.

In the late 1880s, El Pasoan Eldridge Amos Stuart, a grocer, came to the realization that spoiled milk was causing children to become ill. He worked on a new process that sterilized evaporated milk and made El Pasoans healthier. Eventually, Stuart partnered with John Baptist Meyenberg and supplied the Klondike gold miners with evaporated milk. (Courtesy of University of Texas at El Paso, C. L. Sonnichsen Special Collections.)

El Paso's unsympathetic summer heat affected infants. They could easily suffer from dehydration. The lack of refrigeration did not help. Whole milk was available, but there was no way to preserve it. Spoiled milk caused diarrhea and gastrointestinal diseases, sometimes resulting in death. In the early 1900s, electricity made life easier and healthier. Spears and Miller Ice, located at Dallas and Texas Streets, sold ice refrigerators. Once refrigeration became commonplace, illnesses were greatly reduced.

In this downtown shoe store preparing to open, one can see the floor-to-ceiling stacked shoe boxes covering both walls and the sitting bench. While the library-style ladder on the right is ready for use, the two on the left are not. The tin ceiling and cut-glass adornment at the front entrance and cash register are state-of-the-art for this apparently new business.

The U.S. Border Patrol began more than 75 years ago. In 1904, operating out of El Paso, mounted guards patrolled as far west as California trying to restrict the flow of illegal Chinese immigration. On January 16, 1920, the 18th Amendment prohibited the importation, transportation, and manufacture or sale of alcoholic beverages. With this amendment and the Immigration Acts of 1921 and 1924, the U.S. government rejuvenated its interest in border affairs. (Courtesy of the National Border Patrol Museum, El Paso.)

In 1924, the Immigration Act created the El Paso Border Patrol as a uniformed law enforcement branch of the Immigration Bureau. They originally patrolled New Mexico and three western counties of Texas. The first officers selected came from the old mounted guards and the Civil Services Register for railway mail clerks. (Courtesy of the National Border Patrol Museum, El Paso.)

Smuggling has always been common along the Mexican border. Whiskey bootleggers would steer clear of the bridges and easily cross the Rio Grande anywhere else along the southern border. Pres. Franklin D. Roosevelt combined the Bureau of Immigration and the Bureau of Naturalization into the Immigration and Naturalization Service in 1933. In 1934, the first Border Patrol Academy opened at Camp Chigas, El Paso. (Courtesy of the National Border Patrol Museum, El Paso.)

40

In 1852, El Paso appointed its first sheriff, William Ford. His job was to keep peace among the county's nearly 1,000 inhabitants. El Paso was at one time a stopover for Pancho Villa, William "Billy the Kid" Bonney, and a deadly gunslinger by the name of John Wesley Hardin. In this 1934 photograph, sheriffs attend the West Texas Sheriff's Convention and enjoy a day of barbeque, good conversation, and a little firing range practice.

The El Paso Police Department has existed for more than 120 years. Bordering a nation in which corruption is a way of life, police department history has been checkered with scandals, losses, and, in general, "bad times." Today the El Paso Police Department has reached a societal and policing level that is unequalled in the state of Texas and in the United States.

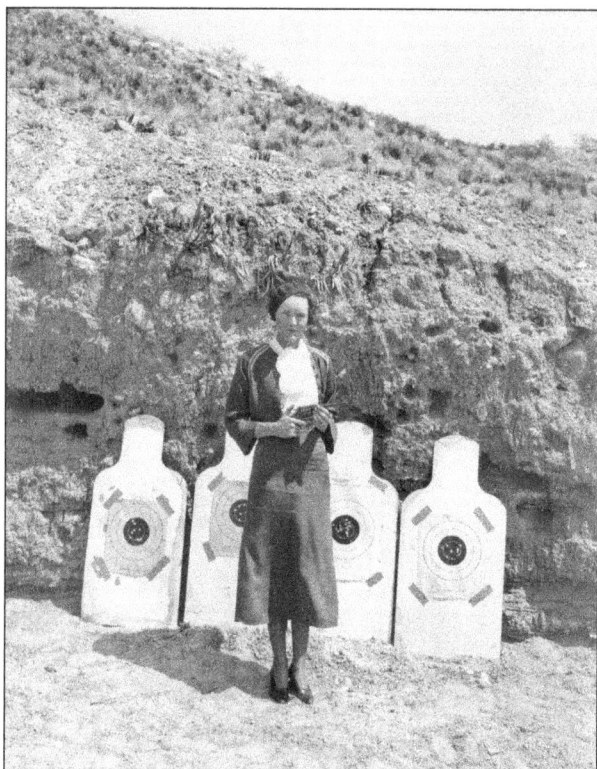

In 1941, the first two women took a test for police clerk. It is unknown whether they became clerks or were ever placed on temporary police duty. It is known that they were never made officers. In 1942, the newspaper published an advertisement for a full-duty policewoman. It was not until 1974 that the first female graduated from the police academy. There were five of them.

In a burgeoning city with a wild reputation like El Paso's, McBean, Simmons, and Carr Undertakers were on call around the clock in 1902. The dusty, rough-and-tumble life along the border meant a steady supply of customers.

Three years prior to the completion of New Mexico's Elephant Butte Dam in 1916, the thought of successfully growing cotton along the Rio Grande was only a probability. In the November 10, 1924, *Christian Science Monitor*, it is noted that the cotton crop was estimated to be worth $10 million. Farmers were reporting more than 73,600 acres dedicated to cotton, twice what it was the year before.

Gathered for this 1910 photograph are, from left to right, (first row) Mrs. Max Weber; Max Weber, German Consulate in Juárez; Elena Arizmendi, founder of the White Cross; Anna Perez, Francisco Madero's wife; Francisco Madero, president of Mexico from 1910 to 1913; and Jose de la Luz Blanco, the Chief of Military of the Plaza; (second row) Fanny Schwartz, Adolph Schwartz's wife; Adolph Schwartz, founder of the Popular Dry Goods Company; and two unidentified. They all benefit from a day together. (Courtesy of University of Texas at El Paso, C. L. Sonnichsen Special Collections.)

The St. Charles Hotel was located at 303½ South El Paso Street. Located on the hotel's ground floor was the Shelton-Payne Arms Company, specializing in firearms, ammunition, sporting goods, and saddlery. Ironically, in this 1916 photograph, the undertaker hangs his shingle next door.

The Globe Department Store was located at 214–218 East Overland Street. I. Laskin was one of the proprietors. The Lenox Hotel occupies the upper floors. Notice that only women surround the store with fashion accessories in the windows.

In 1917, the Myers Company dealt in buggies, wagons, and agricultural implements. It also manufacturered harnesses and saddles. The business was located on the southwest corner of Overland and Campbell Streets. In comparison to the Globe Department Store, there are only men hanging around outside the Myers Company. Right next to the Myers Company store, to the right, at 512 East Overland is the Yellowstone Bar.

El Paso Laundry was owned by W. C. and Crawford Harvie. It was located at 901–909 South Santa Fe Street. In this photograph, El Paso Laundry is pictured before undergoing a renovation in which the white portion was replaced to complement the existing two-story facility.

The B. Farber and Company store is typical even today in downtown El Paso. Millions of Mexicans enter El Paso over the downtown bridges on foot or by vehicle to work, to go to school, and to shop. Several downtown stores, similar to B. Farber, are not managed by Mexicans, Hispanics, or Anglos but rather by El Paso's Korean population. These stores are packed with mostly Mexican shoppers throughout the week.

The *El Paso Times* on June 22, 1952, read, "Elaborate Toltec Club Society's Gathering Place in Early Days": "Those were the days of the nickel beer, with a free lunch thrown in. The man who wasn't bothered by any qualms of conscience could stand before the food counter, holding a glass of beer where everybody could see it, and stuff himself." The list of officers and members includes many who laid the foundation for El Paso.

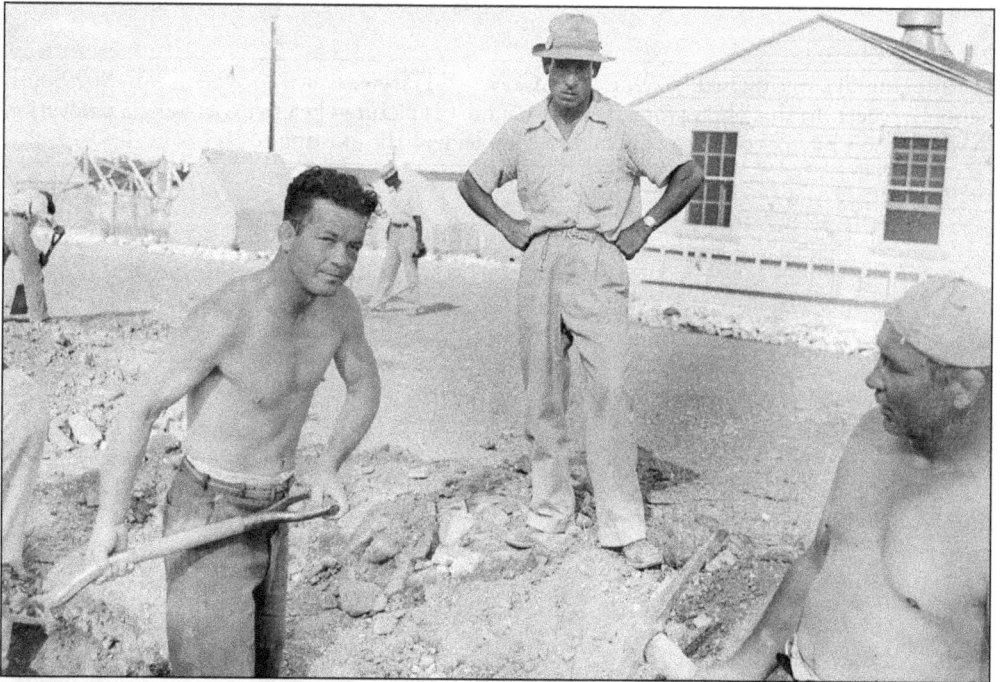

Pauline R. Kibbe writes in her book, *From Latin Americans in Texas*, "Generally speaking, the Latin American migratory worker going into west Texas is regarded as a necessary evil, nothing more nor less than an unavoidable adjunct to the harvest season. Judging by the treatment that has been accorded him in that section of the state, one might assume that he is not a human being at all, but a species of farm implement that comes mysteriously and spontaneously into being coincident with the maturing of the cotton, that requires no upkeep or special consideration during the period of its usefulness, needs no protection from the elements, and when the crop has been harvested, vanishes into the limbo of forgotten things." The League of United Latin American Citizens (LULAC) states, "A best kept secret in American history is that during those years [date not stated] there were more Mexican Americans hung than the total number of blacks hung during the civil war." In the 1950s, El Paso musicians tell stories of traveling west Texas only to arrive at the nightclub and see this sign: "No Niggers, No Dogs, No Mexicans." (Courtesy of University of Texas at El Paso, C. L. Sonnichsen Special Collections.)

Four

ARCHITECTURE

Following the Pueblo Revolt in New Mexico in 1680, Spanish refugees fled south to Paso del Norte and established missions along the Rio Grande. The third and current church in this 1910 photograph at the Nuestra Señora de la Limpia Concepción del Socorro Mission, established in 1682, was completed in 1843 and remains an architectural landmark in the Lower Valley. At one time, the powerful Rio Grande changed its path, placing Socorro, Ysleta, and San Elizario all on an island. Socorro, along with other communities along the river, played a functional role in county politics until the railroads arrived in 1881, shifting political power to El Paso.

The Presidial Chapel of San Elizario (Capilla de San Elcear) was established with the presidio in 1789. The current chapel, completed in 1882, may be the fourth chapel built on or near this site. The curvilinear bell tower, plastered adobe walls, and buttresses serve as outstanding features of typical late adobe church architecture in West Texas and New Mexico in the 1910 photograph.

Since its establishment in El Paso in 1882, the First Baptist Church in this 1884 photograph has been at three locations. The wood-frame church, with its steeply pitched roof and corner tower and spire, located on a triangular lot at Magoffin and San Antonio Avenues, where the Toltec Building currently stands, served the Baptist community until the structure was demolished in 1909.

Otis Aultman's *c.* 1906 photograph of San Francisco Street was taken from Pioneer Plaza, located at that road's intersection with South El Paso Street. Upon the completion in 1908 of the Union Passenger Depot, designed by Daniel Burnam and whose tower is visible in the distance, San Francisco Street ensured its role as the main entry into El Paso. The *El Paso Herald* building, at the foreground on the left, was another early landmark.

One of the oldest extant buildings in El Paso, the First National Bank was constructed in 1882–1883. The first two floors were constructed in the Italianate style, and in 1888, the Second Empire third floor was added. In 1895, the notorious gunfighter John Wesley Hardin briefly occupied one of the second-story rooms as an office for his unremarkable career as an attorney.

The architect S. E. Patton designed the graceful yet solid St. Clement's Episcopal Church in 1906. Patton selected stone from Bedford, Indiana, for the church and the parish house to convey its sense of solemnity. Rev. Henry Easter conducted the first services in the church on Sunday, February 10, 1908.

Beginning in 1899, El Paso's city government operated within this two-story neoclassical structure. Located at San Antonio and Myrtle Avenues, the El Paso City Hall featured a cruciform plan with a central dome. The building replaced the original city hall, which was located at West Overland Avenue and Santa Fe Street. In 1959, the city hall was demolished and its offices relocated.

Henry Trost designed this seven-story reinforced-concrete building for the Rio Grande Valley Bank in 1909. Trost's intention was to reveal the decorative possibilities of concrete as a useful building material. In 1925, El Paso businessman Sam Abdou purchased the building following the bank's defaulting. The quadrilateral site accounts, in part, for the building's distinction of lacking any parallel facades.

Originally known as the Mesa School from its opening in 1889 until it was renamed in honor of pioneer teacher and principal Bessie Bailey in December 1912, the Bailey School was one of the first educational facilities in El Paso. Located at 707 Montana Avenue, the school was acquired by the First Baptist Church in July 1945 and later demolished.

William Ward and Iva Turney commissioned Trost and Trost to design a Classical Revival–style home at 1205 Montana Avenue in 1907. Completed in 1909, the Turney House occupied an entire city block. Palatial and elegant, the Turney House represents one of the largest residences designed by Henry Trost. After 1960, the residence housed the El Paso Museum of Art.

Located at a prominent site near Pioneer Plaza, the White House Department Store and Hotel McCoy in this 1921 photograph exhibits a brilliant employment of the Chicago commercial style. Henry Trost designed this structure to complement the adjacent Anson Mills Building. The department store was housed in the basement and on the first floor, while the hotel was located on the remaining six stories.

Located at 602 North El Paso Street between Missouri and Oregon Streets, the El Paso Lodge No. 130 of the Ancient, Free, and Accepted Masons met for more than six decades at this location. Trost and Trost designed the Masonic Temple in 1912, and its lounge anticipates many of the Southwestern motifs of the firm's later work for the Hotel Cortez (1926) in El Paso and the Hotel Paisano (1930) in Marfa, Texas.

Anson Mills commissioned Henry Trost to design an all-concrete commercial building, which was one of the largest such structures of its kind in the United States upon its completion in 1911. Similar to the White House Department Store and Hotel McCoy, the Mills Building exhibits the influence of Louis Sullivan's Chicago-style architectural language. Trost and Trost located its offices in the Mills Building from its opening until 1920.

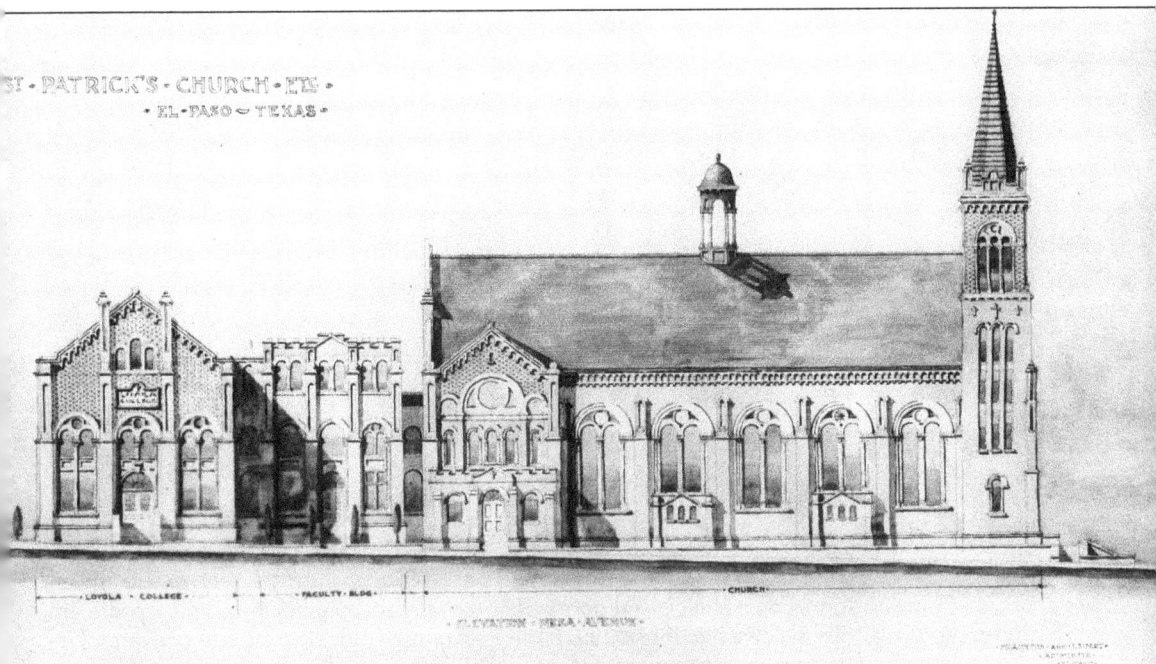

The St. Louis architectural firm of Barnett, Haynes, and Barnett submitted plans for St. Patrick's Cathedral and St. Rita's Chapel in December 1913. Located on the northeast corner of Mesa and Arizona Avenues, the cathedral was dedicated on Thanksgiving Day, November 29, 1917. The combination of Byzantine and Lombard influences characterize this ecclesiastical landmark.

In 1914, Henry Trost's Classical Revival design for El Paso High School harkens to the ancient world of Greece and Rome. The central portico features Corinthian columns and a pediment, and conjoins the two massive building wings. From its mountainside site, the school overlooking the athletic stadium suggests the philosophy of a healthy body in a healthy mind.

The interior of the auditorium features engaged Corinthian columns at the stage and free-standing columns at the rear, and these classical elements link the most prominent interior space with the central portico and the athletic stadium beyond. Drama, like athletics, represents one of the essential aspects of classical civilization, and Trost intentionally incorporated these components into the overall design of the high school.

The philanthropist Andrew Carnegie funded the construction of the El Paso Public Library, which was completed in 1904. It was designed by the St. Louis architectural firm of Mauran, Russell, and Garden, and Gustavus Trost served as field supervisor for the project. The Carnegie Library, the oldest public library in Texas, was located in Buckler Square on the site where the present downtown public library stands.

Henry Trost returned to the Chicago commercial style for the design of the J. J. Newberry Department Store, completed in 1911. Originally occupied by the Calisher's Dry Goods Company, this landmark structure demonstrates that Trost learned much about the art of architecture from his teacher Louis Sullivan, whom he worked for as a draftsman in Chicago from 1887 to 1893.

The inspiration for the Texas School of Mines Administration Building derived from an article on the architecture of Bhutan in the April 1914 issue of *National Geographic* magazine. Kathleen Worrell, the wife of Stephen Howard Worrell, the dean of the School of Mines, believed the similar mountainous landscapes of the Himalayas and the Franklins encouraged the use of Bhutanese architecture, a point of view shared by Trost and Trost in the designs for the first campus buildings.

Ernest Krause designed the original Temple Mount Sinai in 1899 at the intersection of North Oregon and Idaho Streets. Within 17 years, the local Jewish community required a larger synagogue. Trost and Trost designed this massive red-brick temple near the original synagogue at the northeast corner of North Oregon and Montana Streets in 1916.

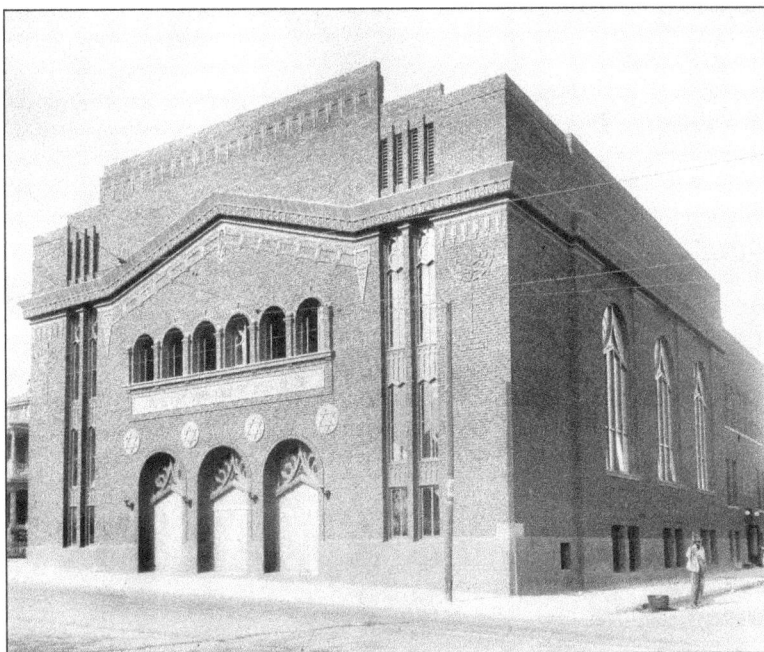

NEW SCOTTISH RITE CATHEDRAL, EL PASO, TEXAS.

Although Trost and Trost prepared a series of renderings for the proposed Scottish Rite Temple in 1916, the commission was ultimately awarded to Hubbell and Greene, an architectural firm in Dallas, Texas. The neoclassical design is emphasized with three entry bays enclosed within two massive pilasters, a dominant cornice, and a strong vertical massing. (Courtesy of University of Texas at El Paso, C. L. Sonnichsen Special Collections.)

Charles N. Bassett commissioned Henry Trost to design this 15-story stepped skyscraper in the moderne and art deco style in memory of his father, Oscar T. Bassett. Selective ornamentation of terra-cotta, granite, art stone, and marble, combined with a powerful vertical emphasis, balance its decoration and massing. Completed in 1930, the O. T. Bassett Tower was Trost's last major work, and one of the facial representations above the main entrance is believed to be a likeness of the architect himself.

Five

MEXICAN REVOLUTION

The meeting of Presidents William Howard Taft and Porfirio Diaz in El Paso and Ciudad Juárez was the first in history between a president of the United States and a president of Mexico. Local press called it the, "Most Eventful Diplomatic Event in the History of the Two Nations." A historian added that it was a "veritable pageant of military splendor, social brilliance, courtly formality, official protocol, and patriotic fervor." The importance of this October 16, 1909, meeting is notably the date; nearly one year prior to the November 20, 1910, beginning of the Mexican Revolution. Diaz accepted Taft's invitation to meet in the El Paso–Ciudad Juárez location because he thought it would reestablish his reputation as a leader who was still in control.

No. 504—Taft-Diaz meeting, El Paso-Juárez, 1909

President Diaz encircled himself with European-educated scholars known as "cientificos." They believed in swift growth for Mexico in spite of the effect it had on the everyday people. By 1910, five percent of the country's population owned all of the land in Mexico. In 1911, El Pasoans were perched on downtown rooftops viewing the Battle of Juárez. Little did they know they were witnessing the beginning of the Mexican Revolution.

José de la Cruz Porfirio Diaz Mori (1830–1915) was a general, politician, president, and dictator. He ruled Mexico from 1876 to 1911. During the Porfiriato, as it was called, tremendous progress took place, and the economy increased substantially. However, only a few benefited. Millions of commoners worked in near-slave conditions. Diaz allowed foreign investment to cultivate Mexico's enormous resources, mainly the United States and Europe. His reign came to an end during 1910–1911 after manipulating an election against Francisco Madero.

Pancho Villa was on the side of the common man and woman. While many regard him as a folk hero, many do not. But most in this west Texas region have a personal story from a relative that has been passed down through the generations relating to an encounter or sighting of Pancho Villa. Villa was responsible for the first attack on U.S. soil since 1812, organizing a raid on Columbus, New Mexico, two hours west of El Paso, in 1916.

Born Doroteo Arango (center right), Pancho Villa's Robin Hood story began after he established himself and his followers in the Sierra between 1900 and 1909. Villa recruited thousands, including Americans. In 1910, Villa and his men, known as *Villistas*, joined Madero's revolutionary forces and ruled over northern Mexico. He even issued his own money. If merchants refused to accept it, they risked being killed. Villa ordered executions at will. They were usually performed by Rodolfo Fierro, or "El Carnicero" (the Butcher) as he was known. (Courtesy of University of Texas at El Paso, C. L. Sonnichsen Special Collections., Franklin Lee Cleavenger Collection.)

Emiliano Zapata (right) was instrumental in bringing down the corrupt dictatorship of Porfirio Diaz in 1911. Prior to this, he was a farmer, horseman, and village leader. Joining forces with other revolutionary generals, they defeated Victoriano Huerta in 1914. Zapata's army was unique in that he allowed women to join the ranks and serve as combatants. He was assassinated in 1919, followed by Venustiano Carranza Garza, who was assassinated in Tlaxcalantongo, Mexico, in 1920. Eufemio Zapata, Emiliano's brother, stands next to him. (Courtesy of University of Texas at El Paso, C. L. Sonnichsen Special Collections.)

Mexican women soldiers were called *soldaderas*. Unfortunately, as is true throughout history, the names and personal information of most *soldaderas* have not been recorded; therefore, they were passed over in history books. There is one *soldadera* whose name lives on in legend, Adelita. There is no official record of Adelita, but her name has become synonymous with courage and heroism. (Courtesy of University of Texas at El Paso, C. L. Sonnichsen Special Collections.)

Women were vital to the Mexican revolution. They participated in the political battlefield, they were powerful voices for just cause, and they wholeheartedly joined the forces on the battlefield. Women were innovative theorists, role models, and, more often than not, fearless. (Courtesy of University of Texas at El Paso, C. L. Sonnichsen Special Collections.)

Francisco I. Madero served as president of Mexico from 1911 to 1913. This improbable revolutionary assisted in the plotting of the overthrow of deep-rooted dictator Porfirio Diaz by initiating the Mexican Revolution. He gathered a group of 200 men, and along with the support of Pancho Villa and Pascual Orozco to the north and Zapata to the south, they forever changed Mexican history. Unfortunately, he was ousted and executed by Victoriano Huerta. (Courtesy of University of Texas at El Paso, C. L. Sonnichsen Special Collections.)

In February 1913, Victoriano Huerta took control of the Mexican government. He served until July 1914. A significant figure in the revolution, he fought against Villa, Zapata, Diaz, and others. Huerta was a heartless fighter and an alcoholic. He was ultimately driven from Mexico and fled to Europe. Upon returning to Mexico through the United States, he was captured and restrained at Fort Bliss, Texas, eventually dying of cirrhosis in 1916. This photograph shows the crowds that gathered in downtown El Paso for his trial.

The Mexican Revolution was fought by a mixture of untrained rebels and professional soldiers. For most of the war, the methods were those of the pre–World War I era. Machine guns were common, rifles were standard—mostly breech-loading magazine-fed repeaters—and the artillery was modern. Of course, there were outdated pieces used by rebels early on. Most armies were composed mainly of cavalry. Being mobile was key.

The Mexican Revolution is one of the only wars of the 20th century to directly impact the United States' mainland. It is estimated that close to 1 million Mexicans were killed during the 10-year war. According to a U.S. Congress report dated February 1915, the Mexican Revolution killed 213 U.S. citizens in Mexico, as well as 36 U.S. citizens inside the United States, most from stray bullets. A total of 92 Mexicans were killed inside the United States. The report was published before Villa's raid on Columbus, New Mexico, where 18 Americans and possibly 50–100 Mexicans were killed. Additionally, 30 U.S. soldiers died on Pershing's expedition to capture Villa.

A short walk from Centro de Trabajadores Agrícolas Fronterizos, where the Border Farmworker Center is now located, lived Mariano Azuela. It was there in 1915 that this doctor, writer, and revolutionary wrote and published *Los de Abajo* ("The Underdogs"), a first-hand description of combat during the Mexican Revolution based on his encounters. He received the National Prize for Literature in 1949. (Courtesy of University of Texas at El Paso, C. L. Sonnichsen Special Collections.)

This was the first of three in a triple execution performed in 1916 at the Juárez train station. The name of the victim is Francisco Rojas, who was a Villista labor organizer. He and his collaborators were killed by Carrancista forces for being supporters of Villa's outlawed movement. Horne, the photographer, wrote in a letter to his wife, "The bullets went right through the man's body. Observe the dust from the wall behind him."

In this unbelievable W. H. Horne photograph shot during the Mexican Revolution, 256 men are hung. What led to this? Whose decision was it? Who executed the orders? Penned on the back of a postcard in period hand, it states, "Just like in the stock yards. Same bunch. This is all Villas work." (Courtesy of the El Paso County Historical Society.)

From left to right, Generals Alvaro Obregon, Pancho Villa, and John J. Pershing, are pictured at Fort Bliss on August 27, 1914, prior to Villa becoming an enemy of the United States. In 1916, Villa ordered 500 troops to attack Columbus, New Mexico. They seized animals, torched a portion of the town, killed soldiers, and stole ammunition and weaponry. President Wilson sent 10,000 troops under Brig. Gen. John J. Pershing, known as the Punitive Expedition, into Mexico. They never caught Villa. However, Pershing was the first to deploy surveillance aircraft in a wartime situation.

The Mexican Revolution was the first true social revolution of the 20th century and one of the bloodiest wars in North American history. One cannot comprehend today's Mexico without referencing the revolution.

One Grave for 63 Men After the Big Battle.

834. W.H. Horne © El Paso, Tex.

Adventurers, businessmen, cowboys, soldiers of fortune, tradesmen, however one refers to them, they all came to Mexico to join in the fight. They were rich, poor, thieves, murderers, and cattle rustlers. They came from all over the globe, but death showed no favoritism, as can be seen in this photograph entitled, "One grave for 63 bodies." Haldeen Braddy called them "a menagerie of international warriors" in his book *Cock of the Walk*.

Back to Camp after a long Dusty Hike.

In the coming months, American soldiers advanced 400 miles into Mexican territory, adapting their maneuvers to a hostile terrain. Unless one has experienced the intense heat of the southwestern sun, one truly cannot imagine what these troops were going through.

El Pasoans sympathized with the ideals of the revolutionaries. Residents walked across the dry Rio Grande taking pictures and selling clothing and food. Dr. Ira Bush served as rebel doctor, establishing a short-term hospital on Campbell Street. According to the *El Paso Times*, a wild bullet killed 20-year-old Vicente Paredes on Santa Fe and Fifth Streets. The Texas National Guard, local law enforcement, and the Texas Rangers guarded the border and the International Bridge.

This photograph represents the hundreds of Mexicans held in El Paso and throughout the Texas borderland, in many cases for their own protection against Villa and other fighting forces in Mexico. It is reported that 100 trainloads of refugees were taken to Fort Bliss. Many lost their children in the mad scramble. (Courtesy of the El Paso County Historical Society.)

The year 1920 generally
symbolizes the end of the
Mexican Revolution. As the
elections approached, Venustiano
Carranza (right) chose not to
run for reelection. Fighting
between rival candidates
continued. Carranza, whose
troops were trying to keep the
peace, was assassinated. Within
a few months, Alvaro Obregon
(below), commanding most of
the federal army, gained the
upper hand, restoring relative
peace. In May 1920, Obregon
was elected president. He
served until new elections in
1924 and peacefully turned
the reins of power over to his
successor, Plutarco Elías Calles.

While driving home from Parral to Canutillo, Pancho Villa (dead, lying across the car door) was assassinated on July 20, 1923, in his Dodge Sedan along with his bodyguards. A street vendor was gesturing to him at the intersection of Benito Juárez and Gabino Barveda. Villa slowed to return the greeting only to have the vendor shout, "¡Viva Villa!" This was a signal for gunmen concealed in a house to open fire. The car crashed into a tree, and Villa was killed instantly. Shortly after Villa's killing, Jesús Salas Barrazas, the congressman for Durango's Eloro district, was charged with the murder. On September 13, 1923, he was sentenced to 20 years in prison. He served six months. Before Barrazas's 1951 death, he confessed to being one of the ambushers. On February 6, 1926, grave robbers cut off and stole Villa's head. It was never recovered. (Courtesy of University of Texas at El Paso, C. L. Sonnichsen Special Collections.)

Six

MILITARY

In 1849, Simeon Hart established Hart's Mill. In 1879, the U.S. government purchased 135 acres, establishing Fort Bliss along the Rio Grande. When Geronimo surrendered in 1886, the government began to eliminate isolated posts and replace them with facilities closer to railroads. El Paso community members purchased more than 1,100 acres on Lanoria Mesa, east of downtown. Fort Bliss moved to its sixth and final home in late 1893.

U.S. Soldiers Camped in the Heart of El Paso, Tex.

In 1848, following orders from the War Department, Maj. Jefferson Van Horne led 257 soldiers, including a howitzer battery, six infantry companies, and the regimental staff, west to El Paso. They arrived in September. The four companies were quartered on Coons' Rancho, formerly Ponce's Ranch, in downtown El Paso. This photograph shows another time when soldiers were quartered downtown.

4.7" Gun Ready to Fire. W. H. Horne Co. El Paso, Tex.

As shown in the W. H. Horne photograph, even with access to 4.7-inch cannons, there was little to protect the soldiers in the open expanse of the Southwest desert.

After the Mexican Revolution, the army increased its troops at Fort Bliss. Eventually 50,000 men were based here. It changed from an infantry station to the largest cavalry post in the United States. Gen. Hugh Scott commanded briefly in 1914, and Gen. John J. Pershing took charge from 1914 through much of 1916. Fort Bliss became Pershing's primary supply base.

Partial excerpts of a letter from Sgt. Sam Avery sent home regarding conditions at Camp Cotton and El Paso in 1916 read, "Although there is no news, for I guess this is the land of nothing, I have to use what time I have in writing. I just received your post cards, and tell Bert I will have to wait until I get home before I buy that gulp [he meant a beer], for this is no place to take a chance. Not for me anyway." (Avery did not want to chance getting drunk and ending up confined.) (Courtesy of University of Texas at El Paso, C. L. Sonnichsen Special Collections.)

A cavalry trooper's horse could carry a maximum of 250 pounds, including the rider. The two- or four-mule wagons carried an astounding 1,200 to 2,400 pounds of cargo. The largest six-mule wagon, itself weighing more than 1,900 pounds, could carry up to 3,300 pounds of cargo. While these slow-moving trains carried a large amount of supplies, they were limited to flat terrain and were almost impossible to hide. (Courtesy of University of Texas at El Paso, C. L. Sonnichsen Special Collections.)

As a general rule, U.S. battle troops performed in agreement with practices learned in the 1889 Spanish-American War and in the Philippines; forces fought using open order formations in front of contemporary small-arms, using the cavalry as mobile infantry. This was true during Pershing's expedition as well. Though some sources vary, U.S. forces make the claim that the use of indirect machine gun fire was invented during fighting the Villistas. (Courtesy of the El Paso County Historical Society.)

In this Mexican Revolution photograph, an American ambulance carries wounded soldiers back to base. The ambulance can carry a maximum of eight wounded.

The Mexican army was no different. In this photograph, the wounded soldiers are taken in a horse-drawn ambulance back across the border into Mexico. Witnesses line the banks of the river. (Courtesy of the El Paso County Historical Society.)

Mass cremation is not uncommon during war time. Field soldiers may not have been able to prepare a mass burial for a large number of dead. Therefore, in order to prevent the spread of disease, bodies were stacked and burned.

The 1st Aero Squadron, the first unit of aviation in the United States, was formed at Fort Sill, Oklahoma. When Villa attacked Columbus, Pershing was soon equipped with six Curtiss JN-2 "Jennies," which had a reputation of being unstable deathtraps. In addition, the air service was handicapped by inexperienced pilots. Pershing was barely a month into the expedition when he lost all of his aircraft. Two crashed within the first week of the expedition. (Courtesy of University of Texas at El Paso, C. L. Sonnichsen Special Collections.)

General Pershing crossed the border at Antelope Pass and set up headquarters at Dublan, Mexico. Pershing's troops protected the colonists from bandits and robbers that preyed upon them. In 1917, Pershing was ordered to return to the United States. More than 1,500 refugees followed Pershing to the United States. (Courtesy of the El Paso County Historical Society.)

Jennies were the first planes to fly into Mexico. They were not equipped with machine guns or bombs; their sole purpose was reconnaissance. Unfortunately for the pilots, the 65-horsepower airplanes did not have the power to fly up and over the Cumbre Pass in Mexico. This spelled certain death. (Courtesy of the El Paso County Historical Society.)

The MB-1 bomber was much larger than the Jennie and was designed to outperform the British Handley Page. It never saw service in the war. However, a number of the bombers were acquired and used by the Post Office Department. (Courtesy of the El Paso County Historical Society.)

A "Rim of the U.S.A. Flight" airplane stands by the MB-1 at the Fort Bliss Flying Field on October 30, 1919. From left to right are Col. Francis W. Glover, USA, Chief of Staff, El Paso Military District; Lt. Col. R. S. Hartz, USA Flight Commander; and Maj. Leo Martin.

Also at Colonia Dublan were Mexican prostitutes. Pershing had the prostitutes placed under guard in a barbed-wire stockade. Soldiers showed the guard on duty that they had the necessary fee regulated by the provost marshal. After visiting with a lady, a soldier was required to take a prophylactic provided by the army. This strict sanitary measure resulted in one of the lowest venereal disease rates an army has ever known. (Courtesy of the El Paso County Historical Society.)

Observation balloons were an early means of military reconnaissance. Balloons were first brought into the army by the Signal Corps in 1865, but this gas bag known as a military observation balloon belonged to the Ohio National Guard and is being used by the Field Artillery at El Paso in 1917.

Quaranteed for Measels.

Measles disables victims for days but usually does not cause death. Texans experienced many epidemics during the 19th century: cholera, dengue fever, diphtheria, influenza, measles, smallpox, whooping cough, and yellow fever. During 1918 and 1919, Spanish influenza affected much of the civilized world. Twenty-five million Americans experienced it, and a half-million died. Some 5,000 cases were reported in El Paso, and 400 deaths occurred.

General Pershing requested that 600 heavy and 1,200 light tanks be produced. Compared to other weaponry, the tank was the most rapidly developed weapon system in the history of warfare, as shown in this 1919 recruiting exhibition at Rio Grande Park in El Paso. The tank was originally designed as a special weapon to solve an unusual tactical situation: the stalemate of the trenches.

Although it does not rain much in the El Paso region, getting stuck during the monsoon season was not uncommon. Notice the dog in the passenger seat.

U.S. Cavalry Drill

W.H. Horne Co.
El Paso, Tex.

Soldiers would perform at military and public events. One trick was to ride around the ring jumping hurdles while standing on the horse's back, "and the horses were moving fast too," according to an 1899 article in the *New York Times*. The soldiers would also jump while riding two horses, one leg on each horse. The most daring trick was with two men standing on the shoulders of two other men took the hurdles.

Seven

SPORTS

Not all that long ago, the traditional art of bullfighting was alive and well in Juárez, Mexico. Tourists from around the world would experience this unique, visual art form at the Plaza de Toros Monumental Bullring during the sport's season, from April through September. Throughout Mexico, it is noted that there are more than 225 bullrings.

Built in 1957, the Monumental Bullring in Juárez held 16,000 spectators. It was the fourth largest bullring in Mexico. Francisco Romero of Ronda, Spain, introduced the *estoque* (sword) and the *muleta* (the small, more easily wielded worsted cape used in the last part of the fight). (Courtesy of University of Texas at El Paso, C. L. Sonnichsen Special Collections.)

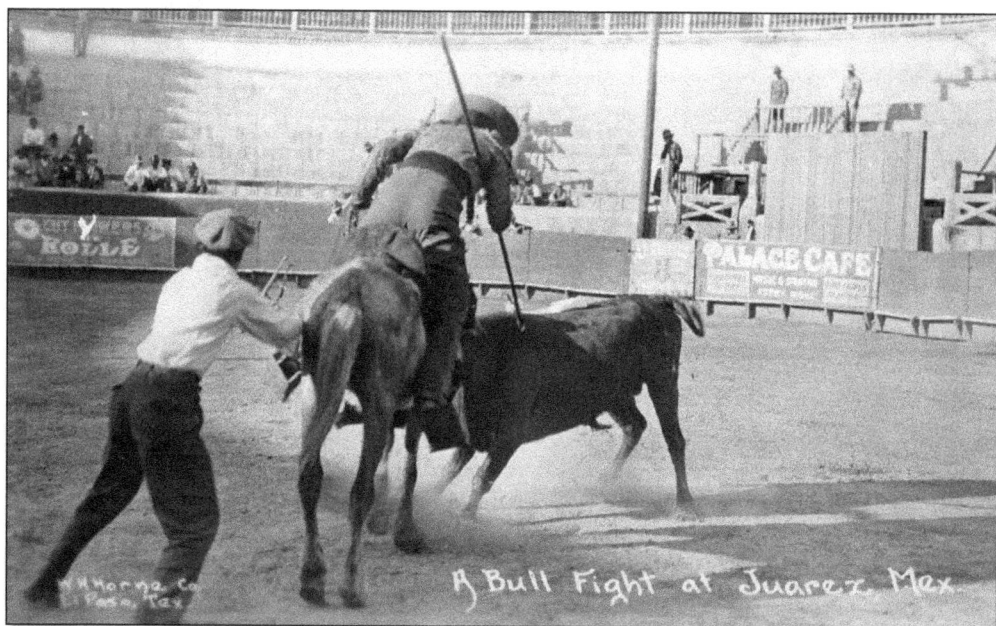

Two picadors armed with a lance circle and joust for position with the bull. The horses are covered with a blanket of sorts, protecting them from the charging bull. It is the picador's job to drive a lance into the neck area, twisting it and thus weakening the bull. While this may not be a pretty sight, it is nonetheless interesting and exciting.

Next, the first of three *banderilleros* run toward the bull. They insert two *banderillas* (adorned wooden sticks with knife ends) over the horns into the bull's neck muscle.

National Sport of Mexico. A Bull Fight at Juarez, Mex.

Finally, the bloodied, dazed bull faces the torero, the principal matador. The torero shows their mastery of the red *muleta* and *estoque*. The matador finishes off the bull by driving the sword down through the neck, instantly killing it.

Bull Killing a Matador

Bullfighting is one of the best known sporting events throughout the world. What young boy or girl has not role-played the mighty matador at one time or another? The origins of the bullring are probably not the Roman amphitheaters but rather Celtic-Iberian temples. In this photograph, a bull finally gets revenge on a matador, killing him. While this rarely happens, bullfighting is an extremely dangerous sport.

In an 1898 *Philadelphia Press* article covering female bullfighters, or señoritas toreros as they are called, it stated, "So novel a sight as six women flirting with a mad bull could not be missed." The audiences were amazed at the skill at which they "handle the sword and banderillas in the great rings of Spain." Some of these talented señoritas toreros were paid handsomely as they toured the republic.

In the 1890s, with the arrival of the railroad, El Paso, like many other Western towns nestled along a railway, became a boomtown. It also developed a reputation as a "Sin City," where plenty of gambling houses, taverns, dance halls, and houses of ill repute dotted the main streets.

Cockfighting is now against the law in the entire United States, but it is still legal in Mexico, where it is also considered a national sport. Breeding of the roosters is not illegal in Texas. The fighting fowls are matched by either age or weight.

"El Paso has had a professional team since 1892," according to Bob Ingram, author of *Baseball from Browns to Diablos.* The baseball team played in Rio Grande Park, built in 1900. The 1913 El Paso Mavericks were part of the Copper League. They went on to win the post-season tournament that same year, becoming the Southwestern champions.

After Rio Grande Park, Dudley Field was built in 1924 and named after Mayor R. M. "Dick" Dudley. In 1951, when the New York Yankees played an exhibition game against the Texans, Mickey Mantle was with them. The Yankees won 16-10. Dudley Field was home to the El Paso team for decades. Dick Azar bought the team in 1954 and brought beer to the park for the first time. (Courtesy of University of Texas at El Paso, C. L. Sonnichsen Special Collections.)

High School Athletics

Rupert W. Gillett, '13

FOOT BALL

The 1911 Season found raw recruits on the field. But the High School spirit was there and before the season was over Coach Coldwell had made a team—a good team—the High School Brand.

The first schedule game was against the Y. M. C. A., a team made up of old High School and College graduates. The "Y" team was heavier and most of the men were veterans, but the Hi held them down to 11-5.

Deming High School vs. El Paso High School, at Deming, was the next battle. El Paso captured the laurels, 40-6.

And then the Tigers met the second team of the N. M. A. C. at Washington Park and vanquished the visitors to the tune of 24-0.

The El Paso Y. M. C. A. again met the Orange and Black warriors, now in their prime. The result was a 12-5 victory for the E. P. H. S.

The Deming High School came to El Paso for a return game, Deming being the only team in the High School class with which the E. P. H. S. did battle during the entire foot ball season. This game resulted in a 60-0 victory for El Paso.

And then came the reaction. A. & M. first team, at Mesilla, easily defeated the High School boys, the final score being 76-0. This result is not surprising when we consider that the Hi boys were playing against a College first team.

A specially prepared second team of the A. & M. avenged themselves at Mesilla, winning from the El Paso boys by a margin of 17 points.

The E. P. M. I. "Varsity" team defeated the High School on Thanksgiving day, ending the season with the score, E. P. M. I. 27, E. P. H. S. 0.

The record:

E. P. H. S.	5	Y. M. C. A.	11
E. P. H. S.	40	D. H. S.	0
E. P. H. S.	24	N. M. A. C. (2nd)	0
E. P. H. S.	12	Y. M. C. A.	5
E. P. H. S.	60	D. H. S.	0
E. P. H. S.	0	N. M. A. C. (1st)	76
E. P. H. S.	0	N. M. A. C. (2nd)	17
E. P. H. S.	0	E. P. M. I.	27
Totals E. P. H. S. 141		Opponents 136	

In the 1911–1912 El Paso High School yearbook, the *Tattler* (sometimes spelled *Tatler* in the yearbook) examines the football team's season performance record: defeating Deming 60-0 and being defeated by (Texas) A&M 76-0. In EP High's defense, A&M is referred to as a "College first" team.

Football Boys

Stanley Shea, '14. Left Halfback.
Seen for the first time this year in an
Orange and Black uniform, "Stuney"
made good as a heavyweight line smash-
er. His punting was a feature of every game; Shea is a strong hope for the
1912 team.

Russell Worthington, '14. Fullback.
Wodthington was a 1911 development, a
good example of what Coach Coldwell
can make out of raw material. He played a hard game all the time, and prom-
ises much for next year.

Henry Blume, '12.. Right Halfback.
This was Blume's first football season;
he played the game "like a demon,"
was one of the fastest men on the team,
and was noted for his ability to gain
yards.

A prime example of three El Paso High Tigers football players is described in this photograph.
As the school song decries, "By the silvery sand of the Rio Grand, the Orange and Black
floats on highs."

102

The Tigers girls' basketball team, known as the Tigress, won the championship in 1912. In the yearbook, it states, "Fresh victims promptly became scarce and not even one more team could be found to meet the H. S. players."

In 1915, John W. "Cap" Kidd donated $800 to equip the State School of Mines and Metallurgy football team, now known as the UTEP Miners. Kidd Field was shared with the UTEP football team until 1962, when the facility became sole home to the track and field team.

In a February 19, 1930, newspaper article by the Reverend Adolf Hoffman, he states, "In 1896, the El Paso Ministerial Association prevented the holding of the Bob Fitzsimmons and Peter Maher championship bout." The fight was originally scheduled for El Paso. The perseverance of the ministers paid off, and the Texas Legislature passed a law prohibiting prizefighting in Texas. Gov. Charles Culberson sent in the Texas Rangers to stop the fight. A couple hundred boxing fans took a train from El Paso to Langtry, Texas, tramped through sand mixed with mud, crossed a pontoon bridge, and eventually reached a crude ring just inside of Mexico. Maher was routed in 1 minute and 33 seconds.

The Irish desperately wanted the championship back. Pancho Villa arranged a fight between Jack Johnson and Jess Willard in Ciudad Juárez. The fight may have netted him something more than mere chump change to carry on his war with Carranza. Carranza let it be known that if Johnson set foot in Mexico, he would arrest him. The location of the fight was changed to Havana, Cuba, where it was fought on April 5, 1915.

In this photograph from April 8, 1921, at the "Punch Bowl Arena" on Fort Bliss, fighters Dick Griffin and Danny Nunes get ready to rumble. The house is packed with mostly well-dressed male boxing fans.

Jack Dempsey, the "Manassa Mauler," is considered by many one of the greatest heavyweights who ever entered in the ring. He was a two-handed fighter who hit hard with both fists. Dempsey was the size of a modern cruiserweight but hit like a super heavyweight. Kid Norfolk, a black heavyweight, clamored for a shot at Dempsey, but Dempsey stated publicly that he would fight only white challengers because the purses were not that large against black fighters.

Dempsey has clearly KO'd his opponent as he walks lightly back to his assigned corner before a sold-out audience. The boxing ring is much larger than the Punch Bowl on Fort Bliss.

DOUBLE MAIN EVENT

WRESTLING

Tues., May 8

OUT OF 3 FALLS—1-HOUR TIME LIMIT

2 OUT OF 3 FALLS—1-HOUR TIME LIMIT

CHEROKEE
—vs—
GI MASK

FELLETTI
—vs—
SEGURA

SEMI-FINAL—2 OUT OF 3 FALLS—45-MINUTE TIME LIMIT

'Gorilla' **POGGI** vs. 'Sailor' **PARKER**

Preliminary **Raul Torres** vs. **Pvt. Jack Hembre** *Ft. Bliss GI* ◀3

serve Your Wrestling Tickets At Shamrock Inn, M-2130; First Nat'l Cigar Stand, M-4838—Prices: $1.10; $1.35; $1.65 Inc. Tax

Liberty Hall, Tuesday, May 8th, 8:30 p. m.

In the early 1900s, two Italian businessmen, Giovanni Reselevich and Antonio Fournier, began promoting fights in which opponents fought hand to hand, without weapons or protection. These fights were known as Lucha Libre, or "free fight." They were notorious for their lack of regulations and violence inflicted upon the *luchadores*, the fighters. In 1929, Salvador Lutteroth González was working in El Paso and began attending professional wrestling matches. It was there that he became fascinated with the sport, especially the colorful personalities of the wrestlers, and decided to bring the sport to his home country of Mexico. The Consejo Mundial de Lucha Libre (CMLL) is the longest running, active professional promotion company in the world. (Courtesy of University of Texas at El Paso, C. L. Sonnichsen Special Collections.)

New Champion

MRS. O. R. ARMSTRONG

Zach White donated 126 acres for the El Paso Country Club to make the Upper Valley attractive to investors. The club opened on January 7, 1922, and featured a swimming pool, double tennis courts, an 18-hole golf course, and horse stables. The clubhouse included a ballroom, a solarium, a ladies card room, a lounge room, open private dining rooms, offices, a screened-in porch overlooking a pool, and a terrace overlooking the golf course.

According to the El Paso County Historical Society *Conquistador*, O. H. Armstrong is "Arguably El Paso's premier woman golfer of the late 1920s and into the 1930s. In 1935 she made history as the first woman to play in a men's tournament in El Paso." In a 1930 *El Paso Times* article, the headline read, "Mrs. Armstrong Sets Record in Defeating Ms. Studley." Armstrong shot a 75, breaking the course record, previously set by her, of 76.

Rodeos and all things cowboy have a magnificent heritage in the state of Texas. Formal rodeo-type competitions date as far back as the 1880s. El Paso played host to the Texas Livestock Association Convention in 1902. Soon business leaders, the Southwestern International Professional Rodeo Cowboy's Association Rodeo, Optimists, Kiwanis, and other clubs began hosting competitions that led to El Paso's beginning of the longest running livestock show in Texas.

In her book, *Behind the Chutes and Elsewhere*, Gail Hughbanks Woerner says Mabel DeLong Strickland looked more like a "Follies Beauty" than a champion cowgirl. She was inducted into the National Cowboy and Western Heritage Museum Hall of Fame, the ProRodeo Cowboys Hall of Fame, the National Cowgirl Hall of Fame, the Pendleton Hall of Fame, and the Cheyenne Frontier Days Hall of Fame. Unfortunately, only the Pendleton induction happened during her lifetime.

Charles K. Hamilton was the most famous aviator of his day. In February 1911, a group of barnstormers calling themselves "birdmen" scheduled the Great International Aviation Meet at Washington Park. Hamilton the year prior had flown the first airplane into El Paso and also claimed the honor of being the first to crash in El Paso.

Katherine "Katie" Stinson was the first woman flier to visit El Paso. She was also the first woman skywriter, the first to perform the loop-the-loop, and the first woman to fly in Canada, Japan, and China. She drove herself and her airplanes to extreme limits, through death-defying stunts, and never suffered a severe crash. Stinson was well respected as a female flier among her male peers.

In 1913, the El Paso YMCA basketball team went undefeated in 28 games, winning the Southwest Championship. According to the photograph, they won "1,000%." Some of the players went on to college.

In 1910, the YWCA of El Paso established a 52-bed residence and gymnasium for young women. The El Paso branch is the largest in the United States and provides services to 201,782 individuals in 17 counties of west Texas and southern New Mexico.

Eight

PEOPLE/BUSINESS/HEALTH

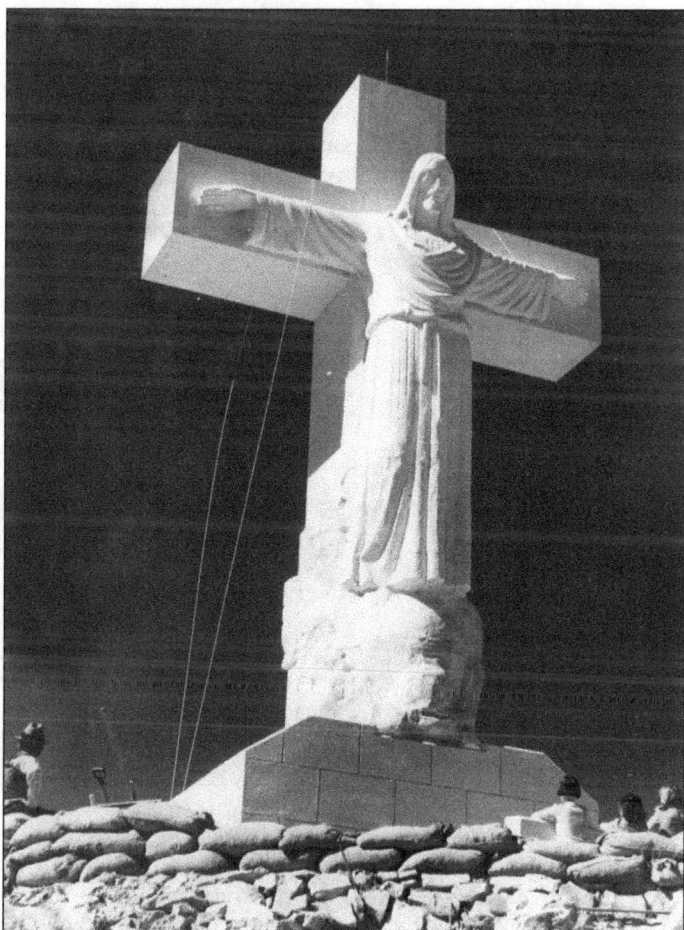

Mount Cristo Rey (Christ the King), a stone monument of Jesus Christ, stands upon a volcanic mountaintop in Anapra, New Mexico, (now called Sunland Park) bordering El Paso. It was inspired by a papal call for mementos of the 19th centennial of Christ. The project was led by Fr. Lourdes Costa, pastor of the Smeltertown parish. Including the base, the piece is 42.5 feet high. Instead of Christ on the cross suffering, Spanish artist Urbici Soler (1890–1953) portrays Jesus with outstretched arms and palms facing down, "in a sublime gesture of peace." It was finished in 1939 and is the largest monument of its kind in North America. (Courtesy of University of Texas at El Paso, C. L. Sonnichsen Special Collections.)

The world's first service-oriented club, the Rotary Club of Chicago, was formed in 1905 by Paul P. Harris. The name "Rotary" came from the exercise of rotating meetings between members' offices. In 1914, sixty-one El Pasoans held a dinner in the Shelton Hotel Cafe to organize a new Rotary Club. In their words, it was to "prepare for a bigger El Paso, this watering station in the middle of the desert."

In his book *Out of the Desert*, Owen White wrote, "All at once educated and refined women who had been reared in Christian and civilized influence, found themselves suddenly transplanted into an atmosphere which literally reeked with the odor of the world, the flesh and the devil." In 1894, Mary H. Mills and 10 other women, including Olga Kohlberg and Mary I. Stanton, registered the Current Topics Club. In 1899, the name was changed to the Woman's Club of El Paso.

Mary Irene Stanton (second from right) received a teaching certificate from North Georgia Agricultural College at Dahlonega, Georgia, and a Bachelor of Science from Austin Female Seminary at Plainville, Georgia. She arrived in El Paso in 1884 and began teaching third grade. In 1894, her own library of 600 volumes was made available. In 1895, the El Paso Public Library Association formed, with her as president. She successfully sought financing from Andrew Carnegie. In 1904, the Carnegie Library opened. Stanton is seen here enjoying a day at the cockfights.

At 16 years of age, in 1887, Kate Moore was the first female graduate of El Paso High. She introduced music into El Paso's public schools, the first such program in Texas. In 1925, she and others founded what is now the El Paso Museum of Art. She and her friends collected fans and shawls from their worldwide travels. These artifacts are now part of the El Paso Museum of History's permanent collection. (Courtesy of the El Paso Museum of History.)

115

Ladies of the day are enjoying a house party in 1898 at the North El Paso Street home of Mrs. Judge Buckner. Among those pictured are (first row) Mrs. W. R. (Kate) Brown and Mrs. Joe Williams; (second row) Kate Hague, Mrs. Zack White, Mrs. James Magoffin, Lucile Hague, Mrs. Judge Buckner, and Mrs. Jack Happer; (third row) Mrs. E. V. Berrian, Mrs. Judge Wilcox, Mrs. J. A. Eddy, Mrs. John Dean, Mrs. Moses Dillon, Mrs. Oscar Baum, Mrs. Max Weber, Mrs. Will Race, Mrs. U. S. Stewart, Mrs. S. T. Turner, and Hattie Race Blumenthal.

In 1940, President Roosevelt ran for a third term. In 1944, he again ran. Democrats believed the nation would become a dictatorship. He supported labor unions and New Deal spending programs. He replaced Vice Pres. John Nance Garner of Texas with Henry Wallace of Iowa. He also established price-fixing on Texas oil. Referred to as the president's "communist" wife, Eleanor Roosevelt enraged Texans with her blunt support for black equality.

116

It is 1900 in this large, wonderfully adorned public kindergarten classroom. The children, while in the middle of a game, are suddenly distracted by something as they all turn and peer. Olga Kohlberg, Margaret True, Mrs. J. E. Townsend, and others convinced the Central School Board to begin a kindergarten class. In September 1893, the first public kindergarten in Texas opened its doors.

In the late 19th century, the only educational requirement to administer a training school for nurses was to be a nurse oneself. Early Texas schools include Hotel Dieu Hospital School of Nursing (1898) and Providence Hospital School of Nursing (1902), both in El Paso. Between 1890 and 1900, the number of training schools nearly quadrupled. Notice there is one man in the above class.

It Is Generally Known—

You can't swim in a pool room.
Remy Hudson is awfully conceited.
Mrs. Warren wouldn't "walk a mile for a camel."
Snowballs don't bounce.
Mosquitoes should not marry.
Paderewski's piano makes a very comfortable bed.
Genevieve Kanen must be 99 44/100 per cent pure.
Jim Dick will be bald-headed before he graduates.
Coach is our school sheik.
Mr. Mottinger heartily endorses ditching.
"Prudent, cautious self-control is wisdom's root."
Sergeant Place *never* gets hard at drill.
Everybody is always on time to assembly.

These truly funny anecdotes can be found throughout the pages of early El Paso yearbooks, year after year. Some, surprisingly enough, are rather risqué, loaded with innuendo. Most are genuinely clever. At the time, the artists and writers must have been well loved—or hated, depending on who they happened to be picking on. The language is simple and surely "hip" for the times.

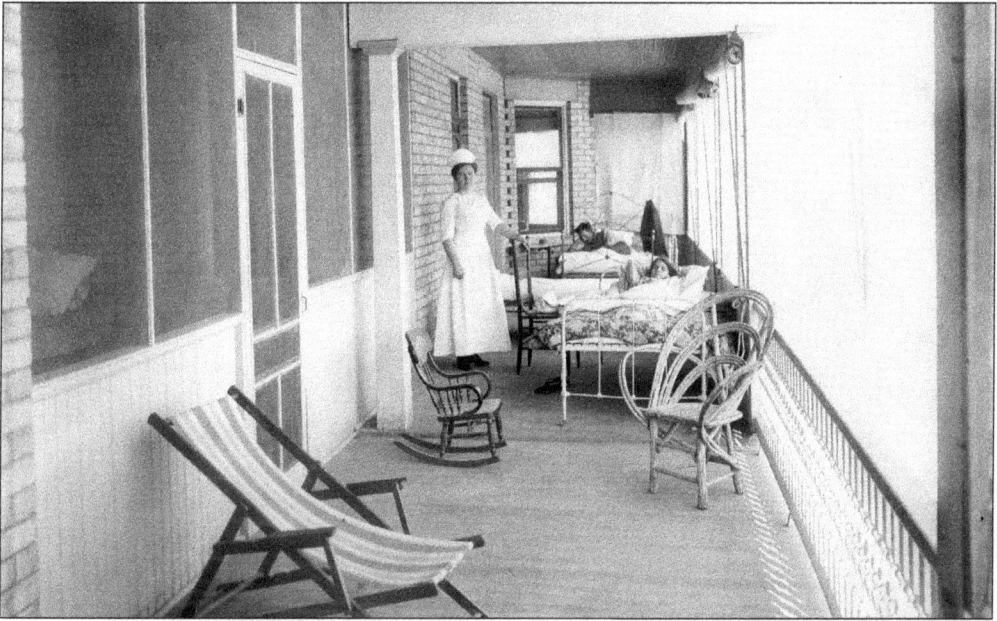

In the 19th century, pulmonary tuberculosis (TB), or consumption as it was called, was thought to be exacerbated by humid air, damp soil, poor eating habits, a lack of exercise, and inadequately ventilated living quarters. Tuberculosis does not discriminate. It has claimed the lives of Eleanor Roosevelt, Vivian Leigh, D. H. Lawrence, Emily Bronte, John Keats, and many more. El Paso was considered ideal for the treatment of TB because of its dry, warm climate.

Two Red Cross vehicles and staff are at hand at a facility with numerous windows and plenty of space. In 1864, the International Red Cross was established by Henri Dunant after his personal relationship with the devastations of war. Clara Barton established the American Chapter in 1881. When Francisco Madero invaded Juárez during the Mexican Revolution, wounded were left lying in the streets. Dr. C. M. Hendricks and others founded the El Paso chapter.

St. Margaret's Home for Children (1919) and the Southwestern Children's Home (1925) were El Paso's first orphanages. During the next 50 years, they cared for thousands of homeless and disadvantaged youth. In 1982, recognizing a similar mission, the two organizations came together as one, creating what is now known as the El Paso Center for Children, expanding and diversifying services to children and families. Their combined mission remains, "A Chance for Every Child." This 1929 Christmas celebration dinner is held in the Hotel Hussmann, originally Hotel Orndorff, and finally in 1934, it became the Hotel Cortez.

Teresa Urrea was a celebrated young healer who it is said helped to inspire revolutionary movements against Porfirio Diaz. Her compassion for the less fortunate was the cause for various uprisings by indigenous communities along the border. While living in El Paso for only two years (1896–1898), she was depicted as the Mexican Joan of Arc. Thousands flocked to her home where she cared for the poor late into the night. (Courtesy of University of Texas at El Paso, C. L. Sonnichsen Special Collections.)

The famous "four dead in five seconds" shootout on April 14, 1881, on El Paso Street, in which Marshall Dallas Stoudenmire shot two of the four while whipping out his twin .44-caliber Colt revolvers, temporarily gave El Paso the name "Six Shooter Capital" until October 26, 1881, when the gunfight at the O. K. Corral occurred.

John Wesley Hardin was named after the founder of Methodism, John Wesley. He claimed to have killed more than 30 men; some say 40. Hardin thought of himself as a pillar of society who killed only to save his own life. He served 15 years in state prison for murder. After his pardon, he opened a law office in El Paso in 1895. He was killed three months later by John Selman, an El Paso city constable. (Courtesy of the El Paso County Historical Society.)

The Beautiful Alice Abbott

Etta Clark and Alice Abbott were business rivals. No one is sure why they became such bitter enemies. At one time, they may have been friends; Abbott had a picture of Clark in her photo album (next page). Gordon H. Frost says in his book *The Gentlemen's Club: The Story of Prostitution in El Paso*, "Venting her anger on the picture, Alice drew an arrow-path into Etta's heart, then caustically accused the petite meretrix with being a 'Whore to Niggers,' the ultimate insult of that prejudiced period." In 1886, Bessie Colvin, one of Abbott's girls, wanted to go work for Clark. The story goes that Abbott followed her and proceeded to bang on Clark's front door. When Clark opened the door, Abbott punched her in the face. Angry, Clark went for a gun, returned and shot Abbot in her groin, resulting in Abbott's demise. (Courtesy of the El Paso County Historical Society.)

122

It was not unusual for a madam to punish her girls for owing money. Etta Clark would confiscate their belongings until repayment was made. This was an efficient way of getting a debt paid back, unless the girls happened to sue their madams. In 1892, Etta Clark's ex-girls claimed she "wrongly appropriated their belongings" and subsequently filed eight lawsuits. Clark lost and had to pay back the girls. (Courtesy of the El Paso County Historical Society.)

According to an *El Paso Herald*, August 28, 1929, article by John R. Whitaker, the Graf Zeppelin arrived in El Paso at 5:13 p.m. The headwinds over Arizona and New Mexico are said to have been the roughest of the "entire world flight." El Paso's Scenic Drive was bumper to bumper with viewers. (Courtesy of the El Paso County Historical Society.)

The Franklin Mountain range is 14.4 miles long and 3.1 miles wide. North Franklin peak is 7,192 feet above sea level. Transmountain Road, cutting between North and South Franklin Peak, is a mile high at its transition point. A temperature difference of 20 degrees between the east and west sides has been noted at times. To visitors, the mountains in El Paso may be quite a pleasant surprise, as one sees from this 1910 photograph. (Courtesy of University of Texas at El Paso, C. L. Sonnichsen Special Collections.)

Yes, it does snow in El Paso. One can expect an average of 4 to 7 inches annually. Normally the mountains get dusted a couple of times. It almost always melts within 24 hours and may never been seen for the rest of the season. That being said, it is always great to see it rain and snow in El Paso because one can rest assured the sun will be out the following day. (Courtesy of University of Texas at El Paso, C. L. Sonnichsen Special Collections.)

Hueco Tanks is just east of El Paso. There are three gigantic granite outcrops rising several hundred feet into the air. It is named for the natural rock basins that capture and hold rainwater. Archaic hunters and foragers from thousands of years ago to recent Mescalero Apaches have drawn more than 2,000 strange, mythological designs on the rocks. There are more than 200 face designs (masks) left by the prehistoric Jornada Mogollon culture.

Spanish explorers brought the first long-horned cattle from the Andalusian Mountains of southwestern Spain. Cortes stocked longhorn cattle on his holdings in Mexico, naming his estate Cuerno Vaca ("Horn Cow"). In 1540, Coronado took 500 head of Spanish cattle on his expedition to find the Seven Cities of Cibola. Some cattle were abandoned and left to run wild. Years later, they numbered in the thousands, becoming the cornerstone of America's legendary Texas longhorn.

REFERENCES

Balderrama, Francisco E., and Raymond Rodríguez. *Decade of Betrayal*. Albuquerque, NM: University of New Mexico Press, 1995.

El Paso Herald Post.

Kibbe, Pauline R. *Latin Americans in Texas*. Albuquerque, NM: The University of New Mexico Press, 1948.

All of the Web sites listed below contained important information about El Paso and/or Texas. But the two that are loaded with goodies and the two that I visited the most are *Borderlands* (www.epcc.edu/nwlibrary/borderlands/) and *Handbook of Texas Online* (www.tshaonline.org/handbook/online/).

www.about.com
www.andalucia.com
www.arago.si.edu
www.articles.directorym.net
www.cbp.gov
www.centralhome.com
www.clubrunner.ca
www.co.el-paso.tx.us/
www.cyberboxingzone.com
www.donquijote.org
www.elpasotexas.gov
www.elpasotimes.com
www.elpasorails.org
www.elprodeo.com
www.emersonkent.com
www.epcc.edu/nwlibrary/borderlands/
www.epccinc.org
www.epcwid1.org
www.epelectric.com
www.epsea.org
www.essortment.com
www.farmworkers.org
www.findarticles.com
www.globalsecurity.org
www.gwpda.org
www.hsgng.org
www.kilgorenewsherald.com
www.ic.arizona.edu

www.latinamericanhistory.about.com
www.loretto.org
www.lulac.org
www.maskalucha.com
www.memory.loc.gov
www.mexconnect.com
www.mexonline.com
www.neta.com
www.netdotcom.com
www.net.lib.byu.edu
www.nytimes.com
www.ojinaga.com
www.over-land.com
www.phudpucker.com
www.rodeoattitude.com
www.rustygunbarrel.com
www.signaturehouse.net
www.spanish-fiestas.com
www.stoppingpoints.com
www.texasbeyondhistory.net
www.texaslonghorn.com
www.tpwd.state.tx.us
www.tshaonline.org/handbook/online/
www.utepathletics.cstv.com
www.ywca.org
www.visitmormoncolonies.com
www.worldwar1letters.wordpress.com

Visit us at
arcadiapublishing.com

· ·

www.ingramcontent.com/pod-product-compliance
Lightning Source LLC
Chambersburg PA
CBHW080626110426
42813CB00006B/1611